THE UNTOLD STORY OF A TEENAGER

(A GUIDE FOR TEACHERS & PARENTS)

NAZIR AHMAD LONE

To my beloved Navodayan Teenagers,

You are the dreamers, the seekers, the artists of life, and the warriors of hope. In your laughter, I have found joy; in your struggles, I have seen courage; and in your stories, I have discovered the essence of humanity.

This book is for you—for every time you dared to dream, even when the world told you not to; for every tear you shed in silence, yearning for understanding; for every step you took forward, despite the weight of doubt and fear.

You have taught me what it means to hope, to fight, and to grow. You have shown me the power of resilience, the beauty of imperfection, and the profound strength of a heart that refuses to give up.

May you always believe in the infinite potential within you. May you never stop dreaming, questioning, or reaching for the stars. And may you always find the love, understanding, and guidance you so deeply deserve.

This book is my tribute to you—my students, my inspiration, my family.

With endless love and pride,
Nazir Ahmad Lone

Contents

Preface   *vii*

  1. Introduction: "Who Am I?"   1

  2. Teachers – The Classroom Perspective   5

  3. Parents – The Home Front   11

  4. Society – The Unseen Observer   17

  5. The Clash Of Expectations   23

  6. Hear Me Out!   29

  7. The Emotional Rollercoaster   35

  8. The Power Of Trust   41

  9. The Need For Freedom And Boundaries   47

10. Building Resilience   53

11. Discovering The Potential   59

12. Contribution To Society   65

13. Conclusion: Understand Me, Nurture Me   71

Preface

There is a story within every teenager—a tale often left untold. It is a story of dreams shimmering with hope, of hearts aching with questions, of battles fought silently, and of an unrelenting search for belonging and understanding. Over the last 18 years, as a teacher and housemaster at Jawahar Navodaya Vidyalayas, I have lived alongside these stories, witnessing them unfold in the laughter, tears, and resilience of countless teenagers.

When a child steps into the corridors of JNV, their eyes glimmer with innocence and boundless possibilities. Their laughter carries the melody of purity, and their questions are like sunlight piercing through the clouds. But as they grow, stepping into the chaotic world of adolescence, their once unclouded eyes begin to reflect a storm—a battle between who they are and who the world expects them to be. Behind their smiles hide unspoken fears, and beneath their bravado lies a yearning: Understand me. See me. Love me for who I am.

The Untold Story of a Teenager was born out of these moments of quiet desperation, unspoken pain, and fragile hope. It is not merely a book; it is a bridge—a heartfelt attempt to connect the world of teenagers with the adults who surround them. Over the years, I have witnessed the clash of expectations between parents, teachers, and society, each demanding a version of perfection that often leaves teenagers lost and fragmented. I have seen their wings clipped by misunderstanding, their dreams crippled by neglect, and their spirits crushed under the weight of relentless expectations.

Yet, amidst the pain, I have also seen remarkable beauty—the resilience of a teenager determined to rise, the creativity that flourishes despite odds, and the boundless love they offer when they feel truly seen. This book is my tribute to them—the dreamers, the fighters, the artists of life who continue to paint their stories despite the odds stacked against them.

Every chapter of this book carries the echoes of real lives—students who stumbled but learned to soar, children whose laughter dimmed under the burden of unmet expectations, and those whose potential shone through the darkness of doubt. It carries the pain of a child who cried silently in the corner of a hostel room, the frustration of a teenager misunderstood at home, and the quiet rebellion of a student dismissed by society. It also carries hope—the kind of hope that flickers in every young heart, waiting for someone to believe in it.

This book is a plea—a heartfelt cry to parents, teachers, and society to pause, to listen, and to empathize. Teenagers are not perfect, nor should they be expected to be. They are explorers navigating the treacherous waters of adolescence, seeking love, understanding, and guidance. They stumble, they fall, and they rise again, but only when someone extends a hand instead of pointing a finger.

To every parent who has struggled to understand their child, to every teacher who has felt the weight of shaping young minds, and to every teenager who has ever felt unseen, unheard, or unloved—this book is for you. It is a call to open hearts, to nurture rather than demand, and to embrace the beautiful chaos of adolescence with patience, compassion, and unwavering belief.

Teenagers are not just our future; they are our present. They carry within them the seeds of change, the courage to dream, and the power to transform. Let us nurture them with care, guide them with wisdom, and love them with all our hearts.

With profound love and hope,
Nazir Ahmad Lone

CHAPTER ONE

INTRODUCTION: "WHO AM I?"

"Teenagers are more than the world sees—more than grades, mistakes, or expectations. They are a delicate soul, navigating emotions, hopes, and the longing to be understood and accepted for who they truly are."

I'm 16 years old, standing on the bridge between childhood and adulthood. It's a tricky place to be—one foot stuck in the innocent world of yesterday, the other desperately trying to step into the world of independence and responsibility. Everyone around me seems to have an opinion about who I should be. But has anyone ever paused to ask me who I really am?

I'm more than a student in a classroom, a child in my parents' home, or a young person in society's gaze. I'm a person with dreams, doubts, and an overwhelming mix of emotions that sometimes I can't even name. My heart yearns to be understood, but instead, I often feel like I'm being dissected, labeled, and judged.

Teachers expect me to excel, to listen, to behave. Parents want me to obey, to succeed, to never falter. Society? Society just wants me to fit into its endless list of rules and roles. Everyone seems to know what's best for me. Yet, I wonder—do they know what it's like to be me?

Here's the truth: I don't need perfection from anyone. I just need to be seen, to be heard, and to be trusted. I'm not asking for my way all the time. I'm asking for understanding—a chance to show that I'm trying my best to make sense of this whirlwind called life.

This book is my attempt to explain what it feels like to be a teenager today. It's about the constant tug-of-war between my own hopes and the expectations of teachers, parents, and society. It's about how I wish to be treated—not with pity or pressure, but with patience and kindness.

In these pages, I'll share my story, my struggles, and my dreams. I'll use analogies to help you step into my shoes and research to show you that my feelings aren't unique—they're part of being human. I'll tell you about the weight of expectations that sometimes feels unbearable, the moments when I wish someone would simply listen, and the times when trust has made all the difference. Through it all, I hope to convince you that teenagers like me aren't problems to be solved. We're potential waiting to be nurtured.

So, who am I? I'm a teenager—a dreamer, a doer, a person who's still figuring it all out. And through this book, I hope to invite you into my world, not to fix me, but to understand me. Because in understanding, we can find connection, and in connection, we can grow together.

Let's start this journey—my story, your perspective, and a bridge between the two.

CHAPTER TWO

TEACHERS – THE CLASSROOM PERSPECTIVE

"Behind every teenage eye-rolling and resistance lies a heart quietly yearning for guidance, trust, and understanding. A teacher's patience and empathy can bridge the gap and ignite the spark of transformation."

I sit in a classroom, staring at the board as the teacher speaks. The words flow over my head, some sinking in, most of them flying past. It's not that I don't care; I do. It's just that sometimes, it feels like my teachers see me only as a number—a grade to be scored, a report card to be filled. But I'm more than that.

Teachers play such a big role in my life. They're not just the people who teach me algebra or chemistry; they're supposed to be mentors, guides, and, sometimes, the ones who help me when I feel lost. Yet, here's the problem: many times, it feels like they forget that I'm not just a student—I'm a person.

In the classroom, I often feel like there's an invisible wall between us. Teachers talk, and I listen, or at least I try. But do they notice when I'm struggling to keep up? Do they see the days when I'm too tired or too distracted to focus? Maybe they do, but they rarely stop to ask why.

The Different Kinds of Teachers
In my experience, there are different kinds of teachers. There are the strict ones, who seem to think discipline is the only way to make us learn. There are the kind ones, who understand that we're not robots but human beings with emotions. And then there are the indifferent ones, who show up, teach, and leave without a second glance.

I don't dislike strict teachers, but I wish they'd realize that yelling doesn't always help. Sometimes, all it does is make me shut down. On the other hand, the kind teachers—oh, how they make a difference! A simple smile or a word of encouragement from them can brighten my whole day.

Analogies: Teachers as Gardeners

If I had to describe teachers, I'd say they're like gardeners. Their job is to nurture us, to help us grow into the best versions of ourselves. But not every plant thrives under the same conditions. Some need sunlight; others need shade. Some need constant watering, while others flourish with just a little care.

Teachers, too, need to understand that each student is different. What works for one might not work for another. Some of us learn quickly, while others need more time. Some of us need encouragement, while others need a little push.

The Good Moments

There have been times when a teacher has made me feel seen, and those moments mean the world to me. Like the time my science teacher stayed back after class to explain a concept I didn't understand. Or the time my English teacher praised an essay I'd written, telling me I had a talent for words.

These small acts of kindness stay with me because they show that my teachers see me as more than just another student. They see me as a person with potential.

The Not-So-Good Moments

But then there are the other moments—the times when a teacher has scolded me in front of the whole class for not knowing an answer, or when they've dismissed my question as "silly." Those moments hurt because they make me feel small and insignificant.

What I Wish Teachers Knew

If I could tell my teachers one thing, it would be this: I want to learn, but I also want to be understood. I'm not perfect, and I'll make mistakes. But those mistakes aren't signs that I'm lazy or careless—they're signs that I'm trying.

I wish teachers would ask, "How can I help you?" instead of saying, "Why didn't you do better?" I wish they'd focus on what I'm doing right instead of only pointing out what I'm doing wrong.

Research: The Impact of Teacher-Student Relationships

Psychologists like Carl Rogers have emphasized the importance of unconditional positive regard in relationships, including those between teachers and students. When teachers show that they care, students are more likely to engage, participate, and succeed. Studies also show that students who feel supported by their teachers tend to have better academic outcomes and higher self-esteem.

The Bigger Picture

I know teachers have their struggles too. They deal with large classes, endless paperwork, and the pressure to produce results. But sometimes, I wish they'd remember why they became teachers in the first place. Wasn't it to inspire, to guide, and to make a difference?

Because when a teacher believes in me, it makes me believe in myself. And when that happens, there's no limit to what

I can achieve.

So, dear teachers, I'm asking for just one thing: See me, not just as a student, but as a person. Teach me, not just facts and formulas, but how to believe in myself. And most importantly, help me grow, not into what you think I should be, but into the best version of who I am.

PARENTS – THE HOME FRONT

"Teenagers don't need perfect parents; they need present ones—ready to listen without judgment, guide with empathy, and love unconditionally as they find their own way."

At home, life feels different from the classroom, but the pressure remains. My parents love me—I know that. They work hard to give me everything I need, and they always say they want the best for me. But sometimes, their love feels like a heavy weight on my shoulders.

You see, parents don't just want us to succeed; they want us to be perfect. Perfect grades, perfect behavior, perfect decisions—everything has to be just right. And when it's not, the disappointment in their eyes cuts deeper than any words ever could.

I'm not saying they're wrong to want the best for me. But I wish they'd understand that I'm not a finished product. I'm still figuring things out, and I need space to make mistakes, to learn, and to grow.

The Different Kinds of Parents

In my world, there are different kinds of parents. Some are like hawks, always watching, always ready to swoop in at the first sign of trouble. Others are like elephants, protective and nurturing, but sometimes overbearing. And then there are the ones who seem like they're barely there, too busy or too tired to pay attention.

I know my parents fall somewhere between the hawks and the elephants. They care deeply, but their care sometimes feels like control. They ask about my studies, my friends, my future—always with good intentions—but rarely about how I'm feeling.

Analogies: Parents as Architects

If I had to describe parents, I'd say they're like architects. They're designing my future, laying down the foundation, and building walls to protect me. But sometimes, I feel like I'm not part of the blueprint. They're planning my life without asking what I want.

What they don't see is that I'm not a building—I'm a seed. I need room to grow in my own way, to find my own path, even if it's different from the one they envisioned for me.

The Good Moments

There are moments when my parents make me feel like the luckiest person alive. Like when they cheer for me at a school event or when they take time out of their busy lives to sit and talk, really talk, without any lectures or judgments.

I remember once, after a particularly hard day at school, my mum hugged me and said, "It's okay to have bad days. You're doing your best, and that's all that matters." That simple moment of kindness stayed with me because it reminded me that their love is bigger than their expectations.

The Not-So-Good Moments

But there are other moments too—times when their words feel like knives. "Why can't you be more like your cousin?" or "Do you even care about your future?" Those words linger in my mind, making me doubt myself.

Sometimes, I wish they'd see how hard I'm trying, even when I fail. I wish they'd understand that comparison doesn't motivate me; it only makes me feel less than I am.

What I Wish Parents Knew

If I could tell my parents one thing, it would be this: I need your love, but I also need your trust. Trust that I'm capable of making good choices, even if I stumble along the way.

I wish they'd stop seeing my mistakes as failures and start seeing them as lessons. I wish they'd ask me what I want, instead of assuming they already know. And most of all, I wish they'd remember what it was like to be my age—to feel confused, scared, and unsure of the future.

Research: Parenting Styles and Teenage Development

Psychologists like Diana Baumrind have studied parenting styles extensively. She identified three main types: authoritarian, permissive, and authoritative. Research shows that the authoritative style—a balance of high expectations and high support—is the most effective for teenagers.

When parents set clear boundaries but also show warmth and understanding, teenagers are more likely to thrive. They feel secure enough to explore their independence while knowing they have a safety net to fall back on.

The Bigger Picture

I know my parents want what's best for me. They've sacrificed so much to give me opportunities they never had. But sometimes, their love feels like a map with only one route, and I'm afraid of taking a wrong turn.

What I wish they'd see is that my journey doesn't have to look like theirs. I have my own dreams, my own passions, and my own way of navigating the world. And with their support—not their control—I know I can achieve amazing things.

So, dear parents, I'm asking for just one thing: Walk with me, don't lead me. Teach me, don't push me. And most importantly, believe in me, even when I struggle to believe in myself.
Because in the end, I don't need you to be perfect. I just need you to be there—patient, loving, and understanding—as I figure out who I am and who I'm meant to be.

CHAPTER FOUR

SOCIETY – THE UNSEEN OBSERVER

"Teenagers are not problems to be solved but potentials to be nurtured; when society listens to their voices and invests in their dreams, it paves the way for a brighter future."

Society is like a shadow that follows me everywhere. It doesn't speak directly, but its presence is always felt. It watches, judges, and sometimes whispers expectations in my ear—expectations that seem impossible to meet.

The funny thing about society is that it's everywhere and nowhere at the same time. It's in the aunt who asks, "What are you planning to do after school?" It's in the neighbors who compare me to their children. It's in the unspoken rules about what I should wear, how I should behave, and what I should aspire to become.

Unlike my teachers or parents, society doesn't have a face. It's a collection of voices, stares, and expectations that shape how I see myself and the world. And yet, it feels like society knows everything about me—my grades, my hobbies, even what I post online.

The Different Faces of Society

Society has many faces. Sometimes it's encouraging, like when people cheer for my achievements. Other times, it's critical, like when they point out my flaws or failures. And then there are times when society feels indifferent, ignoring my struggles because they don't fit the narrative it wants to tell.

There's the supportive society—the one that celebrates talent, applauds hard work, and encourages dreams. But there's also the judgmental society—the one that labels, stereotypes, and criticizes without understanding the full story.

Analogies: Society as a Mirror

If I had to describe society, I'd call it a mirror. But this mirror doesn't reflect who I truly am. Instead, it shows a distorted image, shaped by opinions, biases, and expectations.

Sometimes, society's mirror makes me feel proud, like when it recognizes my efforts and praises my success. But more often, it magnifies my flaws and minimizes my achievements, leaving me feeling inadequate and insecure.

The Good Moments

There are times when society's influence feels positive, like when people come together to support a good cause or celebrate a collective achievement. Moments like these make me feel like I'm part of something bigger, something meaningful.

I remember a community event where I performed on stage. The applause and encouraging words afterward made me feel seen and valued. It was a reminder that society isn't always about judgment—it can also be about connection.

The Not-So-Good Moments

But then there are the darker moments—the times when society feels like a giant weight pressing down on me. Like when I'm judged for not fitting into a certain mold or when my choices are questioned because they don't align with "what's expected."

I've been told, "Boys don't cry," as if showing emotion makes me weak. I've heard, "Girls shouldn't be so ambitious," as if aiming high is something to be ashamed of. These words stick with me, shaping how I see myself and what I believe I'm allowed to do.

What I Wish Society Knew

If I could tell society one thing, it would be this: I'm not perfect, and I shouldn't have to be. I'm a teenager, trying to navigate a world that's constantly changing. I need space to grow, to make mistakes, and to find my own path.

I wish society would stop defining success in such narrow terms. Not everyone will be a doctor, engineer, or scientist. Some of us will be artists, athletes, or entrepreneurs. Success isn't a one-size-fits-all concept, and I wish society would celebrate diversity instead of conformity.

Research: The Impact of Societal Expectations

Psychologists like Erik Erikson have studied the effects of societal pressure on teenagers, highlighting the importance of identity formation during adolescence. When society imposes rigid expectations, it can hinder self-discovery and lead to feelings of inadequacy.

Studies also show that societal support plays a crucial role in building self-esteem. Teenagers who feel accepted and valued by their community are more likely to develop confidence and resilience.

The Bigger Picture

I know society isn't a single entity; it's a collection of people, including my teachers, parents, neighbors, and peers. And while it often feels overwhelming, I also see its potential for good.

Imagine a society that uplifts instead of judges, that listens instead of labels. A society that encourages individuality, embraces diversity, and creates opportunities for everyone to thrive.

Dear society, I'm asking for just one thing: Let me be me. Support me, guide me, and inspire me, but don't box me in. Recognize that I'm still growing, still learning, and still discovering who I am.

Because when society believes in us teenagers, it gives us the courage to dream bigger, try harder, and contribute to the world in meaningful ways. And isn't that what society should be about—building a better future, one person at a time?

CHAPTER FIVE

THE CLASH OF EXPECTATIONS

"When parents demand success, teachers seek discipline, and society expects perfection, the teenager stands at the crossroads, yearning for understanding, guidance, and the freedom to grow into their true self."

Sometimes, I feel like I'm standing in the middle of a battlefield, caught between three armies—teachers, parents, and society. Each one has its own banner, its own rules, and its own expectations of who I should be. And while they all claim to want the best for me, their expectations often collide, leaving me confused, frustrated, and torn.

The Teacher's Expectation

From my teachers, the expectation is clear: Be disciplined, work hard, and excel academically. They see potential in me, and they want me to realize it. But sometimes, their focus on grades and performance makes me feel like a machine, programmed to produce results.

I want to learn, to grow, to understand the world around me. But when learning becomes a race, I start to lose sight of why I'm running in the first place. I wish they'd see that I'm more than just my marks—that my worth isn't measured by percentages or ranks.

The Parent's Expectation

My parents, on the other hand, want me to be everything they couldn't be. They want me to succeed, not just for myself but for the family, for our name, for our pride.

Their expectations aren't just about academics; they're about character, behavior, and choices. They want me to be respectful, responsible, and obedient. And while I understand their intentions, their expectations sometimes feel like chains, binding me to a future I didn't choose.

The Society's Expectation

And then there's society, the silent observer with the loudest voice. It doesn't care about my individuality; it cares about how I fit into its mold.

Society expects me to conform, to follow its unwritten rules, and to meet its standards of success and propriety. It tells me what I should study, how I should dress, and even who I should aspire to be.
But what society doesn't see is how suffocating these expectations can be. They don't leave room for creativity, curiosity, or individuality.

The Clash

The real struggle begins when these expectations overlap—and contradict each other.
My teacher might tell me to focus on academics, but my parents might insist I help out with family responsibilities.

My parents might encourage me to follow a traditional career path, but society might glorify something entirely different.

And while society praises academic toppers, it also celebrates influencers and celebrities, sending me mixed signals about what success really means.
I often feel like I'm being pulled in different directions, trying to please everyone but ending up pleasing no one.

Analogies: The Tug-of-War

If I had to describe my life, I'd call it a tug-of-war. Teachers, parents, and society are all pulling me toward their side, and I'm the rope, stretched thin and frayed at the edges.

But what they don't realize is that this constant tugging doesn't make me stronger. It makes me weaker, more uncertain, and more afraid to take a step in any direction.

The Emotional Toll

The clash of expectations isn't just a battle of ideas; it's a storm of emotions.

I feel guilty when I can't meet my parents' expectations.
I feel frustrated when my teachers don't see my struggles.
I feel invisible when society overlooks my individuality.

These emotions weigh on me, creating a sense of inadequacy that's hard to shake.

What I Wish They Knew

If I could speak to all three—the teachers, the parents, and society—I'd ask them to pause for a moment and listen. Listen to what I want, what I need, and what I'm capable of.

I'd tell them that their expectations, while well-meaning, often feel like burdens. I'd ask them to work together, not against each other, to help me grow into the best version of myself.

Research: The Impact of Conflicting Expectations

Studies in developmental psychology reveal that conflicting expectations can lead to increased stress and anxiety in teenagers. Psychologist Albert Bandura emphasized the importance of self-efficacy—the belief in one's ability to succeed. When expectations clash, this belief is often undermined, leaving teenagers feeling lost and demotivated.

Experts suggest that a supportive and collaborative approach from all stakeholders—teachers, parents, and society—can help teenagers navigate their challenges more effectively.

The Bigger Picture

The clash of expectations isn't just my struggle; it's a universal teenage experience. But it doesn't have to be this way.

Imagine a world where teachers, parents, and society work together, aligning their expectations to support the individual needs of every teenager. A world where they see us not as projects to be completed but as people to be nurtured.

Dear teachers, parents, and society, I'm not asking you to lower your expectations. I'm asking you to align them. To trust me, guide me, and believe in me as I navigate this journey of self-discovery.

Because when expectations don't clash, they can become a source of strength—a foundation that helps me grow, thrive, and find my place in the world.

CHAPTER SIX

HEAR ME OUT!

"Every teenager silently pleads, 'Listen to me—not to judge or correct, but to understand who I am and the world through my eyes."

"Why doesn't anyone listen to me?" That's a question I find myself asking more often than I'd like. It feels like my voice gets lost in the noise of instructions, advice, and criticism. Everyone around me—teachers, parents, and society—seems so eager to tell me what to do, but no one pauses to ask me what I think or how I feel.

And when I do try to speak, my words are often dismissed. "You'll understand when you're older," they say. Or worse, "You're just being dramatic." But I'm not being dramatic. I'm being me—a teenager with thoughts, emotions, and dreams that are just as real as anyone else's.

Why Listening Matters

Listening isn't just about hearing words; it's about understanding feelings. When someone truly listens to me, it makes me feel valued, respected, and supported. It's like they're saying, "You matter, and what you have to say is important."

But when my voice is ignored or silenced, it sends a very different message: "Your thoughts don't count. Your feelings aren't valid. Your opinions don't matter." And that hurts more than words can explain.

The Conversations I Crave

There are so many things I wish I could say if only someone would listen.

To my teachers, I'd say: "I'm not just a student; I'm a person. Please see me as more than just a roll number or a report card."
To my parents, I'd say: "I know you want the best for me, but sometimes your best feels like too much. Can we find a balance?"
To society, I'd say: "Stop telling me who to be and start asking me who I want to become."

Analogies: The Echo Chamber

Sometimes, it feels like I'm trapped in an echo chamber. I hear everyone else's voices—loud, clear, and constant—but mine barely registers. And the more I try to speak, the more my voice gets lost in the cacophony.

What I long for is a conversation, not a lecture. A space where my voice isn't just heard but also understood and valued.

Moments of Silence

There have been rare moments when someone truly listened to me—really listened.
Like the time my teacher asked, "What do you think?" and waited patiently for my answer. Or the day my parent said, "I'm sorry, I didn't realize this was hard for you." These moments stand out because they're so rare, but they mean everything to me.

When someone listens to me, it feels like a light turning on in a dark room. It gives me clarity, hope, and the courage to keep speaking, even when it feels like no one's listening.

The Power of Empathy

Listening isn't just about hearing words; it's about understanding emotions. When someone listens with empathy, it makes me feel seen—not just as a teenager, but as a person with unique experiences, struggles, and dreams.

Empathy says, "I'm here with you. I may not have all the answers, but I care about what you're going through." And sometimes, that's all I need.

Research: The Psychology of Being Heard

Psychologists like Carl Rogers emphasize the importance of active listening in building trust and fostering emotional well-being. According to research, teenagers who feel heard are more likely to develop self-esteem, resilience, and a sense of belonging.

Listening also strengthens relationships, creating a foundation of mutual respect and understanding. It's a simple act with profound effects.

What I Wish for

If I could make one wish, it would be this: Let me speak, and truly listen when I do.

I'm not asking for constant attention or agreement. I know I'll make mistakes, and my ideas won't always be perfect. But I need the freedom to express myself without fear of judgment or dismissal.

The Bigger Picture

Listening isn't just about me; it's about building connections. When teachers, parents, and society take the time to listen, they create a space where I feel safe, supported, and understood.

And when I feel heard, I'm more likely to listen in return. To my teachers, parents, and society, I'll say this: Your voices matter to me, too. But the best conversations are the ones where we both get to speak—and truly hear each other.

So please, hear me out. Not just today, but every day. Because when you listen to me, you're not just hearing my words; you're helping me find my voice. And that voice, when nurtured, can change the world.

CHAPTER SEVEN

THE EMOTIONAL ROLLERCOASTER

"A teenager's heart is an emotional rollercoaster—soaring with dreams, plunging with doubts, and twisting with questions—yearning for someone to ride along with patience and understanding."

Being a teenager feels like riding a rollercoaster blindfolded. The highs are exhilarating, the lows are crushing, and the twists come out of nowhere. Emotions I can't always explain crash over me like waves, leaving me exhilarated one moment and overwhelmed the next.

Some days, I feel invincible, like I can conquer anything. Other days, I feel like I'm barely holding it together. It's confusing, exhausting, and sometimes lonely. But it's also real—it's my life, my journey, my emotional landscape.

The Spectrum of Emotions

I wish I could tell you what it feels like to be me, to live with emotions that seem to have a mind of their own.

Joy: When I laugh with my friends or accomplish something I've worked hard for, I feel like I'm flying.
Fear: When I think about the future or worry about failing, fear grips me like a shadow I can't escape.
Anger: Sometimes, I get angry, not because I want to, but because I don't know how else to express my frustration.
Sadness: There are moments when sadness creeps in, making me feel small and invisible.
Love: And then there's love—not just romantic love, but the love I feel for my friends, my family, my passions. It's powerful, consuming, and beautiful.

Why It Feels So Intense

The truth is, I don't always understand why I feel the way I do. Science tells me it's because my brain is still developing—particularly the parts that control emotions and decision-making.

But knowing this doesn't make it any easier. Sometimes, it feels like my emotions are a storm, and I'm just trying to stay afloat.

The Pressure to Hide

What makes it harder is the pressure to hide what I'm feeling. Society tells me to "toughen up," my parents tell me to "stop overreacting," and sometimes even my friends tell me to "chill."

But suppressing my emotions doesn't make them go away. It just buries them deeper, where they simmer and grow until they eventually boil over.

Analogies: The Volcano Within

If I had to describe my emotions, I'd call them a volcano. Most of the time, they're dormant, bubbling beneath the surface. But every now and then, the pressure builds, and they erupt—sometimes in anger, sometimes in tears, sometimes in silence.

The eruption isn't the problem; it's the buildup that hurts the most. What I need is a way to release the pressure before it overwhelms me.

Moments of Understanding

There have been times when someone truly understood what I was feeling—when a teacher noticed I was struggling and offered a kind word, or when a friend listened without judgment.

These moments stand out because they remind me that I'm not alone, that my emotions are valid, and that it's okay to feel deeply.

What I Wish Others Knew

I wish teachers, parents, and society knew that my emotions aren't a sign of weakness. They're a sign of growth, of learning, of becoming.

To my teachers, I'd say: "When I'm upset in class, it's not because I don't care. It's because I'm overwhelmed. A little patience can go a long way."

To my parents, I'd say: "When I seem moody or withdrawn, it's not because I'm pushing you away. It's because I'm trying to figure out how to cope."

To society, I'd say: "When I express my emotions, don't tell me to 'get over it.' Help me navigate them instead."

Research: The Teenage Brain and Emotions

Psychologists like Dr. Daniel Siegel explain that the teenage brain is wired for emotional intensity. The amygdala, responsible for processing emotions, is highly active during adolescence, while the prefrontal cortex, which helps regulate emotions, is still maturing.

This isn't a flaw; it's a feature of being a teenager. It's what allows us to feel deeply, take risks, and form strong connections. But it also makes us more vulnerable to emotional turbulence.

Finding Balance

What I've learned is that emotions aren't something to fear or suppress. They're a part of who I am, a part of what makes me human.

What I need isn't for my emotions to disappear; it's for others to help me understand and manage them.

The Bigger Picture

Emotions are like the waves of the ocean—sometimes calm, sometimes stormy, but always moving. And just like the ocean, they're a source of beauty, power, and life.

To my teachers, parents, and society, I ask this: Don't judge me for my emotional rollercoaster. Ride it with me. Be my anchor in the storm, my guide through the waves.

Because when you help me navigate my emotions, you're not just helping me survive the ride—you're helping me find my way to solid ground. And for that, I'll always be grateful.

CHAPTER EIGHT

THE POWER OF TRUST

*"Trust is the foundation of a strong bond with a teenager;
when a teacher or parent shows trust, they inspire the
teenager to believe in themselves and strive for their best."*

Trust—it's such a small word, but it carries the weight of the world. For me, trust is the bridge between who I am now and who I aspire to become. It's the invisible thread that binds my relationships with my teachers, my parents, and society.

But trust isn't something you can demand or decree. It's something you earn, nurture, and protect. And for teenagers like me, trust is the difference between feeling empowered and feeling isolated.

What Trust Means to Me

To me, trust means believing in someone and knowing they believe in me. It's the assurance that I can share my thoughts, make mistakes, and be vulnerable without fear of judgment or betrayal.

- **With my teachers**, trust means knowing they see me as more than a grade or a discipline problem. It means feeling safe enough to ask questions or admit when I don't understand something.
- **With my parents**, trust means knowing they'll guide me without controlling me, that they'll allow me the freedom to grow while being there to catch me if I fall.
- **With society**, trust means believing that I have a place, that my voice matters, and that my efforts can make a difference.

When Trust is Broken

Unfortunately, trust is fragile. It can take months or years to build but only moments to break.

- When a teacher calls me out in front of the class instead of addressing me privately, I feel embarrassed and exposed.
- When my parents dismiss my dreams as unrealistic or impose decisions without considering my perspective, it makes me feel unheard and undervalued.
- When society stereotypes teenagers as reckless, lazy, or incapable, it undermines my confidence and motivation.

Broken trust doesn't just hurt; it creates walls—walls that are hard to break down once they're built.

The Trust Cycle

Trust is a two-way street. When I feel trusted, I'm more likely to act responsibly and rise to expectations. But when I feel mistrusted, I either withdraw or rebel—it's a natural response to feeling unappreciated.

It's like a plant. If you water it with trust, it grows and flourishes. But if you neglect it or poison it with doubt, it withers.

Analogies: The Tightrope Walker

Trust, to me, feels like walking a tightrope. With the right balance of support and freedom, I can make it across, step by step.

- If the rope is too loose (excessive leniency), I'll fall.
- If the rope is too tight (overbearing control), I won't be able to move forward.

- But when the rope is just right, I can navigate it with confidence, knowing there's a safety net below.

Moments of True Trust

I've experienced moments when trust felt like magic.

Like the time my teacher entrusted me with a class project and praised my leadership, even when I made mistakes. Or the time my parents gave me the freedom to choose my path, even though they had their doubts.

These moments taught me that trust isn't about perfection; it's about faith. Faith in my intentions, my abilities, and my potential.

What I Wish Others Knew

Trusting me doesn't mean letting me do whatever I want. It means guiding me while believing in my ability to learn and grow.

- **To my teachers,** I'd say: "When you trust me, I feel inspired to do better—not because I have to, but because I want to."
- **To my parents**, I'd say: "When you trust me, it shows me that you believe in me, and that belief gives me the courage to believe in myself."
- **To society,** I'd say: "When you trust me, you remind me that I have the power to make a positive difference."

Research: The Psychology of Trust

Psychologists like Erik Erikson emphasize the importance of trust in adolescence. According to his stages of development, teenagers need a balance of autonomy and guidance to build a sense of identity and confidence.

Research also shows that teenagers who feel trusted by adults are more likely to exhibit self-discipline, take responsibility, and maintain healthy relationships.

The Building Blocks of Trust

So how can teachers, parents, and society build trust with teenagers like me?

1. **Listen without judgment:** Sometimes, I just need to be heard.
2. **Show consistency:** Keep your promises and be reliable.
3. **Respect my individuality:** Acknowledge that my journey may look different from yours.
4. **Encourage mistakes:** Let me learn and grow without fear of harsh consequences.
5. **Express belief in me:** Your confidence in me fuels my own confidence.

The Bigger Picture

Trust is more than a relationship; it's a foundation. When you trust me, you're not just giving me freedom—you're giving me the tools to become the best version of myself.

And when I feel trusted, I'm more likely to trust in return. I'll trust your guidance, your wisdom, and your intentions. Together, we can create a bond that empowers both of us.

So, to my teachers, parents, and society, I ask this: Trust me. Not blindly, but with hope, patience, and belief.

Because when you trust me, you're not just shaping my future—you're shaping the future of the world.

CHAPTER NINE

THE NEED FOR FREEDOM AND BOUNDARIES

"Teenagers thrive when given the freedom to explore and the boundaries to stay grounded—it's in this balance that they discover their strength and direction."

As a teenager, I long for freedom—the space to explore, to dream, to make decisions, and yes, even to make mistakes. But at the same time, I understand the importance of boundaries. They're like the guardrails on a mountain road: they keep me safe while allowing me to move forward.

The tricky part is finding the balance between the two. Too much freedom feels overwhelming, like being set adrift with no direction. Too many boundaries feel suffocating, like being locked in a cage. What I need is a harmonious blend—a guiding hand that lets me grow while ensuring I don't fall too far.

Why Freedom Matters

Freedom is the air I breathe. It's what allows me to explore who I am and who I want to become.

- **Freedom to choose**: Whether it's picking my subjects, hobbies, or friends, having a say in my life makes me feel valued.
- **Freedom to make mistakes:** Mistakes aren't failures; they're lessons. When you let me stumble, you're giving me the chance to learn resilience and responsibility.
- **Freedom to express myself:** Whether through art, writing, or simply voicing my opinions, self-expression helps me process my emotions and thoughts.

When I'm given freedom, I feel trusted, respected, and capable. It's a powerful feeling, one that motivates me to rise to the occasion.

Why Boundaries Matter

But freedom without boundaries is like a kite without a string—it might soar for a moment, but it'll eventually crash. Boundaries give me structure, security, and a sense of right and wrong.

- **Boundaries provide clarity:** They help me understand what's acceptable and what's not, guiding me to make better choices.
- **Boundaries protect me:** They shield me from dangers I might not yet recognize.
- **Boundaries teach discipline:** They remind me that freedom comes with responsibility.

When boundaries are clear and fair, they don't feel like restrictions; they feel like care.

The Clash Between Freedom and Boundaries

The tension between freedom and boundaries is where most of the conflicts in my life arise.

- **With my parents:** They want to protect me, but sometimes their rules feel like chains.
- **With my teachers:** They want to discipline me, but sometimes their methods feel harsh or inflexible.
- **With society:** It sets expectations for how I should behave, but often forgets to respect my individuality.

What I wish for is a middle ground—a space where my freedom is respected but still guided by reasonable boundaries.

Analogies: The Garden and the Fence

If my life were a garden, freedom would be the sunlight and rain that help me grow. Boundaries would be the fence that keeps out the weeds and predators.

Without the fence, the garden would be vulnerable to destruction. But without the sunlight and rain, it wouldn't thrive. Both are essential, and both must coexist.

Moments of Balance

There have been times when I've experienced the perfect balance between freedom and boundaries.

- Like when my teacher gave me the freedom to choose a project topic but set clear deadlines and expectations.
- Or when my parents let me go out with friends but asked me to check in at certain intervals.
- Or when society celebrated my individuality without labeling me or imposing stereotypes.

These moments taught me that freedom and boundaries aren't opposites—they're partners.

What I Wish Others Knew

I wish my teachers, parents, and society understood that I don't want absolute freedom or rigid control. I want a balance.

- **To my teachers,** I'd say: "Trust me with independence, but guide me with clear instructions."
- **To my parents,** I'd say: "Let me spread my wings, but be there to catch me if I fall."
- **To society,** I'd say: "Allow me to challenge norms and think differently, but remind me of my responsibilities."

Research: Freedom, Boundaries, and Adolescent Development

Psychologists like Dr. Laurence Steinberg emphasize that adolescents thrive in environments that combine warmth, structure, and autonomy. Authoritative parenting—marked by high acceptance, supervision, and psychological autonomy granting—has been shown to produce confident, responsible, and self-disciplined individuals.

Similarly, in education, giving students some control over their learning while maintaining structure fosters engagement and creativity.

The Recipe for Balance

So, how can freedom and boundaries coexist in harmony?

1. **Communicate**: Let me know the reasons behind rules and expectations.
2. **Negotiate**: Be willing to adapt boundaries as I grow and prove my responsibility.
3. **Empower**: Give me opportunities to make decisions and learn from their outcomes.

4. **Support**: Be there to guide me when I stumble, without taking away my autonomy.

The Bigger Picture

Freedom and boundaries aren't just about controlling or protecting me; they're about preparing me for the world. When you balance the two, you're teaching me to navigate life with confidence, respect, and responsibility.

To my teachers, parents, and society, I ask this: Give me the freedom to explore, the boundaries to stay safe, and the trust to find my way.

Because when you strike the right balance, you're not just helping me grow—you're helping me thrive.

CHAPTER TEN

BUILDING RESILIENCE

"Resilience isn't built in isolation; it's cultivated through challenges, supported by encouragement, and strengthened by the belief that every fall leads to a stronger comeback."

Life is not a straight path; it's a series of winding roads, steep climbs, and occasional detours. For a teenager like me, every challenge feels monumental, every failure feels final, and every stumble feels like the end of the world. But deep within, I know resilience is the key to navigating these ups and downs.

Resilience isn't just about bouncing back; it's about growing stronger with every setback. It's the inner strength that keeps me moving forward, even when the odds seem stacked against me.

What Resilience Feels Like

Resilience, to me, feels like a spark that refuses to go out, even in the stormiest weather.

- It's the courage to face a tough exam after failing the last one.
- It's the strength to rebuild friendships after conflicts.
- It's the determination to keep trying, even when my confidence wavers.

Resilience is my shield, protecting me from self-doubt and despair.

Challenges That Test My Resilience

Teenage life is filled with challenges that push me to my limits:

- **Academic pressures:** The constant race for grades and achievements can feel overwhelming.
- **Social dynamics:** Navigating friendships, peer pressure, and conflicts can leave me feeling vulnerable.
- **Family expectations:** Balancing my dreams with my parents' aspirations is a delicate dance.
- **Society's judgment:** Living up to societal stereotypes of success and behavior can be suffocating.

Each challenge feels like a test of my strength and patience, but it's also an opportunity to grow.

Resilience in Action

I've experienced moments where resilience has carried me through.

- Like when I worked tirelessly to improve in a subject I once struggled with, and the effort paid off.
- Or when I stood up to peer pressure, even though it meant feeling isolated for a while.
- Or when I faced criticism but chose to learn from it instead of letting it define me.

These moments taught me that resilience isn't about avoiding difficulties—it's about embracing them.

Analogies: The Bamboo and the Oak

Resilience reminds me of bamboo. Unlike the mighty oak, which might crack under pressure, bamboo bends with the wind but doesn't break. It sways, adapts, and survives the storm.

In the same way, resilience isn't about being unyielding; it's about being flexible. It's about bending without breaking, adapting without losing yourself.

What Helps Me Build Resilience

Resilience isn't something I'm born with; it's something I develop, with the help of those around me.

- **From my teachers:** Encouragement and constructive feedback teach me to learn from mistakes.
- **From my parents:** Unconditional support and belief in my abilities help me rebuild confidence.
- **From society:** Opportunities to contribute and grow instill a sense of purpose and self-worth.

Every kind word, every second chance, every bit of faith helps me build my resilience.

What I Wish Others Knew

Resilience isn't about pretending to be strong or hiding my struggles. It's about acknowledging my challenges and finding the strength to rise above them.

- To my teachers, I'd say: "Help me see failures as stepping stones, not roadblocks."

- To my parents, I'd say: "Guide me through tough times, but let me fight my own battles too."
- To society, I'd say: "Create spaces where I can learn, grow, and bounce back without fear of judgment."

Research: The Psychology of Resilience

Dr. Ann Masten, a leading resilience researcher, calls resilience "ordinary magic"—a set of natural abilities and supports that help individuals adapt to adversity. Studies show that resilience in adolescents is fostered by strong relationships, positive role models, and opportunities to build competence.

Steps to Building Resilience

So how can teenagers like me develop resilience?

1. **Cultivate a growth mindset:** Believe that challenges are opportunities to grow.
2. **Build strong relationships:** Lean on trusted adults and friends for support.
3. **Practice self-compassion:** Be kind to yourself when you fail or falter.
4. **Focus on solutions:** Instead of dwelling on problems, look for ways to overcome them.
5. **Set realistic goals:** Break big challenges into manageable steps.

The Bigger Picture

Resilience isn't just about surviving; it's about thriving. It's the foundation for success, happiness, and fulfillment.

To my teachers, parents, and society, I say this: Help me build resilience. Encourage me to face challenges, support me when I fall, and celebrate with me when I rise.

Because with resilience, I'm not just preparing for the storms of teenage life—I'm preparing for the storms of life itself.

CHAPTER ELEVEN

DISCOVERING THE POTENTIAL

"Teenagers are like seeds bursting with untapped potential—nurture them with belief, guide them with care, and watch them grow into something extraordinary."

As a teenager, I'm often caught in a whirlwind of emotions, expectations, and self-doubt. It's easy to lose sight of who I am and what I'm capable of. Yet, deep inside, there's a spark—a potential waiting to be discovered, nurtured, and unleashed.

Discovering my potential is not just about figuring out what I'm good at; it's about understanding who I am, what I value, and how I can contribute to the world. It's about believing that I have something unique to offer, even when the world feels overwhelming.

The Journey of Self-Discovery

Discovering potential is like exploring uncharted territory—it's thrilling, daunting, and full of surprises.

- **My interests:** Whether it's art, science, sports, or music, the things that excite me are clues to my potential.
- **My strengths:** Recognizing what I'm naturally good at boosts my confidence and helps me set meaningful goals.
- **My values:** Understanding what matters most to me gives direction to my efforts.
- **My dreams:** Dreaming big allows me to envision a future that aligns with my passions and aspirations.

Every moment of self-discovery feels like uncovering a hidden treasure.

Challenges Along the Way

The path to discovering potential isn't always smooth. It's filled with obstacles that can make me doubt myself.

- **Fear of failure:** What if I'm not as good as I hope to be?
- **Comparisons:** It's hard not to measure myself against others and feel inadequate.
- **Pressure to conform:** Society often pushes me to follow a predefined path, even if it doesn't align with my interests.
- **Limited opportunities:** Sometimes, I don't have the resources or guidance to explore my talents fully.

These challenges can cloud my vision, making it harder to see my potential.

Moments of Realization

There have been moments when I caught glimpses of my potential—moments that inspired me to keep going.

- When a teacher recognized my skill in writing and encouraged me to join a competition.
- When my parents celebrated my creativity, even if it was just a simple drawing.
- When a friend believed in my abilities, even when I didn't.

These moments reminded me that potential isn't just about talent; it's about perseverance, support, and self-belief.

Analogies: The Hidden Seed

Discovering potential is like nurturing a seed. At first, it's invisible, buried beneath the soil. But with the right care—sunlight, water, and time—it grows into a tree, bearing fruits and offering shade.
The seed holds infinite possibilities, but it needs the right environment to thrive.

How Others Can Help

Discovering potential isn't something I can do alone. Teachers, parents, and society play a crucial role in helping me realize what I'm capable of.

- **Teachers**: Inspire me to explore new ideas, challenge me to push my limits, and guide me with patience and encouragement.
- **Parents**: Support my passions, celebrate my efforts, and remind me that my worth isn't tied to my achievements.
- **Society**: Create opportunities for me to learn, grow, and contribute without fear of judgment.

When you believe in me, you ignite my belief in myself.

What I Wish Others Knew

Potential isn't always obvious. Sometimes, it's hidden behind fear, inexperience, or lack of confidence.

- To my teachers, I'd say: "Help me see what I can't yet see in myself."
- To my parents, I'd say: "Encourage me to explore, even if the path seems uncertain."
- To society, I'd say: "Value my unique abilities, not just the ones that fit the norm."

Research: Nurturing Potential in Adolescents

Dr. Carol Dweck's research on the growth mindset highlights that believing in one's ability to improve is key to unlocking potential. Adolescents thrive when they are encouraged to see challenges as opportunities for growth rather than threats to their self-worth.

Steps to Discovering Potential

So how can I uncover and nurture my potential?

1. Explore: Try new things, even if they seem intimidating at first.
2. Reflect: Take time to think about what excites and fulfills me.
3. Set goals: Start small, build momentum, and aim high.
4. Seek feedback: Listen to those who believe in me and learn from constructive criticism.
5. Stay resilient: Understand that growth takes time and setbacks are part of the journey.

The Bigger Picture

Discovering potential isn't just about achieving success; it's about becoming the best version of myself. It's about finding my place in the world and making a difference in my own way.

To my teachers, parents, and society, I say this: Help me explore, believe in my dreams, and guide me when I falter. Because when you support my journey, you're not just helping me find my potential—you're helping me shape the future.

CHAPTER TWELVE

CONTRIBUTION TO SOCIETY

"Teenagers are the architects of tomorrow's society—shaped by their dreams, fueled by their passions, and driven by the belief that they can create a better world."

As a teenager, I often wonder: what can someone my age contributes to society? Can my thoughts, actions, or dreams make any difference in a world so vast and complex? These questions linger in my mind, but deep down, I believe that each of us, no matter how young, has something valuable to offer.

Society isn't just a structure I live within; it's a community I can shape. My generation carries the potential to bring fresh perspectives, innovative ideas, and boundless energy to the table. All I ask is for you to trust me, guide me, and show me how I can make a difference.

How Teenagers Can Contribute

Teenagers may not yet have the experience of adults, but we have a unique set of qualities that allow us to make meaningful contributions:

1. **Ideas and Creativity:** We see the world through fresh eyes, unburdened by traditional constraints. From tech innovations to creative art, our ideas can inspire change.
2. **Energy and Passion:** When we believe in something, we put our hearts into it. Be it a local cleanup drive, a social media campaign, or raising awareness for a cause, our enthusiasm can spark movements.
3. **Empathy and Compassion:** Growing up in a connected world makes us more aware of global issues. Whether it's volunteering, donating, or advocating, we want to help where we can.
4. **Adaptability and Tech Savviness:** Born in a digital age, we're quick to adapt and innovate. Our tech skills can be

used to solve problems, raise awareness, or create new opportunities for others.

What Stops Us from Contributing?

Despite our willingness to contribute, we often face barriers that hold us back:

- **Doubt**: Society sometimes underestimates us, assuming we lack the wisdom to make a real impact.
- **Lack of Platforms:** Opportunities to lead or participate meaningfully in social initiatives are often limited for young people.
- **Pressure:** With academics and personal expectations weighing heavily on us, it can be challenging to find time and space to contribute.

We don't ask for much—just a chance to prove what we can do.

Moments of Impact

There are moments when I've felt the power of contribution:

- Helping an elderly neighbor with technology.
- Organizing a charity event in school for underprivileged children.

- Standing up for a friend being bullied and promoting kindness in my circle.

These experiences showed me that contribution doesn't have to be grand to be meaningful.

Analogies: The Ripple Effect

Contributing to society is like tossing a pebble into a still pond. The ripples may start small, but they grow outward, touching distant shores.

As a teenager, my actions may seem insignificant, but they can inspire others, creating a chain reaction of kindness, innovation, and positive change.

How Teachers, Parents, and Society Can Help

Our contributions often need nurturing and guidance. Here's how you can help us:

- Teachers: Show us how our skills can be used to benefit others. Encourage us to think beyond textbooks and apply our knowledge in real-world contexts.
- Parents: Support our passions, even if they seem unconventional. Teach us the value of giving back and lead by example.
- Society: Provide platforms for us to engage—youth forums, volunteer opportunities, or community projects where our voices are heard and valued.

What I Wish Others Knew

Our contributions might not solve world hunger or end global conflicts, but they are steps toward a better tomorrow.

- To my teachers, I'd say: "Teach me to use my learning for good."
- To my parents, I'd say: "Believe in my ability to make a difference."
- To society, I'd say: "Recognize my efforts, no matter how small they seem."

Research: Teenagers as Agents of Change

Studies in developmental psychology highlight how engaging teenagers in community service fosters a sense of purpose and responsibility. According to Dr. Richard Lerner, a leading expert in adolescent development, teenagers who are encouraged to contribute to their communities exhibit higher self-esteem and better mental health.

Steps Toward Contribution

Here's how I, and teenagers like me, can start making a difference:

1. **Identify Passions:** Find causes or areas that resonate with our values and interests.

2. **Take Initiative: Start small**—helping a neighbor, volunteering at school, or creating awareness online.
3. **Collaborate:** Work with friends, teachers, or community leaders to amplify our impact.
4. **Learn:** Understand societal issues deeply before jumping in, so our efforts are meaningful.
5. **Stay Committed:** Real change takes time, so perseverance is key.

The Bigger Picture

Teenagers are not just the future; we are the present. Our voices matter, our ideas matter, and our contributions matter.

To my teachers, parents, and society, I say this: Empower me. Show me that my actions, no matter how small, can create a ripple of change. When you trust me to contribute, you're not just building a better society—you're building a confident, capable individual ready to take on the world.

Because when we all contribute, together, we can create a world that's brighter, kinder, and more inclusive.

CHAPTER THIRTEEN

CONCLUSION: UNDERSTAND ME, NURTURE ME

"They long to be understood with compassion and nurtured with patience, as they strive to grow into the person they are meant to become."

As I conclude my story, I hope it has shed light on what it feels like to be a teenager navigating a world shaped by teachers, parents, and society. My journey is not unique—it echoes the experiences of millions of teenagers striving to find their place, their voice, and their purpose.

If there's one message I wish to leave behind, it is this: **understand me, nurture me, and help me grow**

Understanding Me

Understanding a teenager requires more than observing our actions; it demands delving deeper into our emotions, thoughts, and struggles.

- **When I rebel:** It's not defiance; it's my way of asserting independence.
- **When I withdraw:** It's not indifference; it's my need to process overwhelming emotions.
- **When I make mistakes:** It's not incompetence; it's my opportunity to learn and grow.

Understanding me means seeing beyond my words and actions to the unspoken feelings beneath. It's about empathy, patience, and the willingness to meet me halfway.

Nurturing Me

Nurturing me doesn't mean sheltering me from challenges or solving all my problems. It's about equipping me with the tools, confidence, and support to navigate life's complexities.

- **Give me guidance, not control:** Show me the path, but let me take my steps.
- **Celebrate my efforts, not just my successes:** Every attempt I make is a step toward growth.
- **Be my anchor, not my leash:** Let me explore the world while knowing I can always return to your steady presence.

The Role of Teachers, Parents, and Society

You, as my teachers, parents, and society, are the pillars that shape me. Each of you plays a vital role in my development, and your actions leave lasting impressions on my heart and mind.

- **Teachers:** Teach me not just facts but values. Inspire me to think critically, dream boldly, and act compassionately.
- **Parents:** Be my unwavering support. Balance your expectations with understanding, and trust my ability to find my way.
- **Society:** Accept me for who I am. Provide opportunities for me to contribute and grow, and recognize the potential within my youthful spirit.

The Vision of Tomorrow

When you understand me and nurture me, you're not just shaping a teenager—you're shaping the future. A future where young minds are empowered to innovate, empathize, and lead. A future where teenagers like me feel valued, understood, and inspired to give back to the world.

My Promise

In return, I promise to:

- **Learn from you:** I will take your wisdom and make it my foundation.
- **Challenge myself:** I will strive to grow, improve, and fulfill my potential.
- **Contribute to society:** I will use what I learn to make a positive difference in the world.

Final Thoughts

I am not perfect, and I don't expect you to be either. But together, we can create a relationship built on trust, respect, and mutual understanding.

To my teachers, parents, and society, I say this: **Stand by me, guide me, and believe in me. Your understanding and nurturing can transform my teenage struggles into stepping stones for success.**

Because with your support, I can grow into a person who not only fulfills your dreams but also creates my own—a person who contributes meaningfully to a world we all share.

Thank you for hearing my story. Now, let's write the next chapter together.